The Queen's Quilt

Written by
Jill Atkins

Illustrated by
Andy Hamilton

Queen Jonquil met King Quentin in the garden. She had a quick chat with the king.

"Quentin, I wish you to join me for quoits. But my silver quoit is missing. Will you look for it?"

Quentin shook his jacket.
"Yes, I will go and look for it now."

"Good, Quentin. But you cannot quit until you get it. Be quick!"

King Quentin ran to the tower.

He zoomed up and down,
but he did not see the quoit.

Then he ran to the river.

A duck was near the river.
She was sitting on the quoit.

It was near her bottom.

King Quentin had lots of coins in his pocket.

"Ten quid?"

"Quack!"

The duck took the ten quid.

Quentin took the quoit and ran back to the queen.

But he was not quick and now it was dark.

With a huff and a puff he got to Queen Jonquil. She was in bed.

I fear the king will not join the queen for quoits tonight!